THE DANGERS OF DRUGS, ALCOHOL, AND SMOKING

THE DANGERS OF
VAPING

LISA IDZIKOWSKI

PowerKiDS press
New York

Published in 2020 by The Rosen Publishing Group, Inc.
29 East 21st Street, New York, NY 10010

First Edition

Editor: Jenna Tolli
Book Design: Reann Nye

Photo Credits: Cover Hemant Mehta/Getty Images; series art patpitchaya/Shutterstock.com; p. 5 Ary6/iStock/Getty Images Plus/Getty Images; p. 7 MaryCaroline/Shutterstock.com; p. 9 Leon Neal/Getty Images News/Getty Images; p. 10 Hazem.m.kamal/Shutterstock.com; p. 11 Diego Cervo/Shutterstock.com; p. 13 Richard Baker/In Pictures/Getty Images; p. 15 NicolasMcComber/iStock/Getty Images Plus/Getty Images; p. 16 NurPhotoi/Getty Images; p. 17 Steve Heap/Shutterstock.com; p. 19 mark_vyz/Shutterstock.com; p. 21 Hero Images/Getty Images; p. 22 Monkey Business Images/Shutterstock.com.

Cataloging-in-Publication Data

Names: Idzikowski, Lisa.
Title: The dangers of vaping / Lisa Idzikowski.
Description: New York : PowerKids Press, 2020. | Series: The dangers of drugs, alcohol, and smoking | Includes glossary and index.
Identifiers: ISBN 9781725309944 (pbk.) | ISBN 9781725309968 (library bound) | ISBN 9781725309951 (6 pack)
Subjects: LCSH: Vaping–Juvenile literature. | Electronic cigarettes–Juvenile literature. | Smoking–Health aspects–Juvenile literature. | Youth–Tobacco use–Juvenile literature.
Classification: LCC HV5748.I49 2020 | DDC 362.29'6–dc23

Manufactured in the United States of America

Some of the images in this book illustrate individuals who are models. The depictions do not imply actual situations or events.

CPSIA Compliance Information: Batch #CWPK20. For Further Information contact Rosen Publishing, New York, New York at 1-800-237-9932.

CONTENTS

HAVE YOU SEEN THIS?

Most young people have seen a cigarette, but have you ever seen an electronic cigarette, or "e-cigarette"? Maybe you've noticed someone using one and didn't know what it was. They can look like everyday items, such as pens or flash drives. Using an e-cigarette is called vaping.

Young people can be fooled into thinking these products are safe to use. Many of them attract young people because they taste like fruit or candy. But don't be fooled—they are still harmful. Kids could also get into trouble for using them. In most states, it's illegal for stores to sell them to people under 18.

DANGER ZONE

Unfortunately, e-cigarettes are popular among high school students. In 2018, about one in five high school students used them.

Look closely. E-cigarettes can look like regular cigarettes and sometimes it's hard to tell the difference. E-cigarettes, unlike regular cigarettes, do not burn tobacco.

5

VAPING: WHAT IS IT?

The name "e-cigarette" is short for "electronic cigarette." They are small machines or devices that run on **batteries**. Most devices have a pod that is filled with liquid. When someone smokes the e-cigarette, the liquid heats up. As it gets hotter, it changes into a vapor, which is where the term "vaping" comes from.

When someone vapes, they breathe this vapor into their lungs. To them, it may feel good or taste good. Some young people think it's only water vapor, but it isn't. Actually, it is much more harmful. Vape liquid contains nicotine, a harmful **chemical** that is also in cigarettes.

E-cigarettes are sometimes called e-cigs, vapes, or vape pens. Some look like computer flash drives.

>

7

had different flavors. The device was not popular at the time, and the e-cigarettes used today were invented in China many years later. By 2005, electronic cigarettes were sold around the world.

DANGER ZONE

1963 was a busy year for smokers. In the year the first e-cigarette was invented, Americans smoked over 500 billion cigarettes.

About 55 years after they were invented, e-cigarettes started to become popular across the world. It is now a $10 billion **industry.**

ECIGWIZARD

ECIGWIZARD
SHOP
OPEN

A HARMFUL DRUG

There are many different flavors for e-cigarettes, like candy, fruit, or chocolate. Some of the packages for e-cigarette products even look like food items. They might seem harmless, but they still have very dangerous, or unsafe, chemicals inside them.

The liquid that is heated in e-cigarettes is called e-juice or vape juice.

Don't be tricked—vaping causes problems for kids, teens, and young adults. When people vape, their eyes, throat, and lungs become sore and **irritated**. They could get sick more easily too. E-cigarettes also have ingredients that can increase risks for **cancer**. And sadly, some young people move on to smoking regular cigarettes later. There have even been times when the batteries in e-cigarettes explode or catch on fire!

11

FULL OF CHEMICALS

You might see middle school and high school students outside with clouds of smoke or vapor near them. If you do, watch out! The mist or **aerosol** from e-cigarettes is full of harmful chemicals. At least 60 different chemicals have been found in e-cigarettes, including many that help make the aerosol and the flavorings that can also be dangerous.

E-cigarette products usually contain nicotine, which is the same chemical found in regular cigarettes. This is the chemical that makes smoking cigarettes and vaping so **addictive**. Nicotine has even been found in e-cigarettes that say they are nicotine-free.

DANGER ZONE

By 2018, over 2 million middle and high school students used e-cigarette products. From 2017 to 2018, e-cigarette use by middle schoolers went up by nearly 50 percent.

The vapor from e-cigarettes might look different from cigarette smoke, but it still lets harmful chemicals into the air, like nicotine.

13

that our brains continue to change as we grow. When babies are born, their brains are just starting to **develop**. As we get older, different parts of the brain keep developing until we are around 30.

The chemicals found in e-cigarettes can hurt brain development. When young people use them, it can affect parts of the brain that are still growing. These areas handle learning, attention, and memory. Nicotine also changes certain connections in the brain that can lead to addiction.

Our brain makes connections between cells whenever we learn something new. When young people use nicotine, it changes the way these connections are made.

>

15

DON'T PAY ATTENTION TO THOSE ADS

Companies that make and sell e-cigarettes want people to buy their products. The main way they do this is through advertising. The ads might show happy teenagers, adults, or famous people using e-cigarettes. They are often shown on social media and websites.

DANGER ZONE

In the United States, ads for regular tobacco cigarettes were banned from television and radio in the 1970s. The government is starting to **regulate** advertising for e-cigarettes too.

VIP
MAKE THE SWITCH. VIP CIG

Photon Tank System.

VIP Custom Made and
Designer Blended E-Liquids

Mix and Blend to
Create 80+ Flavours

Companies are clever at making ads. E-cigarette companies can make it seem like using their product is part of everyday life.

That's not all. E-cigarette companies market to young people too. They might try to make e-cigarettes seem cool or high tech. They also **promote** their brands in different ways, like hosting events or concerts. Be in the know! When you see e-cigarette ads, keep in mind that companies are usually trying to find new customers.

ISN'T THERE A LAW?

Unfortunately, many students in middle school and high school are using e-cigarettes. Doctors, teachers, and parents want to help young people understand the dangers of these drugs so they know to stay away from them. But how can they do it? Are there any laws to help?

In 2018, the Food and Drug Administration (FDA) suggested plans to limit the number of teens vaping, including a ban on selling e-cigarette flavors that appeal to kids. Although there are laws against using regular cigarettes in public places, they aren't always the same for e-cigarettes. However, more states are starting to include vaping in these laws too.

DANGER ZONE

The United States government officially announced that e-cigarette use among teenagers is an **epidemic** in 2018. They asked the public to take action and help protect young people from vaping.

NO SMOKING
INCLUDING ELECTRONIC CIGARETTES

Some places also include "no electronic cigarettes" on their signs that ask people not to smoke.

HELP IS OUT THERE

People on social media might make vaping seem cool. You may even begin to see people you know start this dangerous habit. It's important to remember that e-cigarettes contain nicotine which can make it hard for people to stop using them.

Sometimes it can be challenging for young people when they want to quit vaping because there are not as many **treatment** options for people under the age of 18. When young people want to quit using e-cigarettes, they should always talk to their parents or another adult they trust to help.

DANGER ZONE

Some people have said it can be harder to quit vaping than smoking. Some negative effects from trying to quit can include serious mood changes, head pain, and stomach sickness.

Talking to a trusted adult can help young people learn how to quit vaping.

21

STAY HAPPY AND HEALTHY

Adults always want young people to stay happy and healthy. They want kids to stay in school and become successful. Once someone starts to use drugs, especially as a young person, it can be very hard to stop. Vaping and other drugs can lead to addiction and other serious health problems.

Young people don't always know about the dangers of vaping and the chemicals that are inside of e-cigarettes. E-cigarettes might not have all of the same chemicals as regular tobacco cigarettes, but they are always dangerous for young people to use. You can stay safe by keeping away from e-cigarettes and vaping.

GLOSSARY

addictive: Causing someone to be unable to stop using or taking a harmful substance, like a drug.

aerosol: A substance that is kept in a container under pressure and released as a fine spray.

battery: A small device placed inside larger machines to supply them with electricity.

cancer: A serious sickness that can spread to other parts of the body and is caused by cells that are not normal.

chemicals: Matter that can be mixed with other matter to cause changes.

develop: The act of building, changing, or creating over time.

epidemic: A sickness that spreads widely and affects many people at once.

industry: A group of businesses that provide a certain product or service.

irritate: To make sore or painful.

promote: To make people aware of something through advertising.

regulate: To make rules or laws that control something.

treatment: Medical care given to a patient for an illness or an injury.

23

INDEX

WEBSITES

Due to the changing nature of Internet links, PowerKids Press has developed an online list of websites related to the subject of this book. This site is updated regularly. Please use this link to access the list: www.powerkidslinks.com/das/vaping